KATE PETTY is a well-respected writer and editor
of children's books. She is the author of many picture books
including *Made With Love* (Macmillian) and *The Nightspinners*
(Orion). She is currently the commissioning editor for
Cornwall's biodiversity attraction, the Eden Project.
Kate's previous book for Frances Lincoln is *Hair*,
part of the Around the World series.

For Ben and John

Oxfam would like to acknowledge, with thanks, the following photographers:
Annie Bungeroth (pages 5 and 10–11), Howard Davies (pages 24–25 and cover), Julio Etchart (pages 12–13),
Jim Holmes (pages 6–7, 14–15 and 20–21), Ley Honor Roberts (pages 8–9), Crispin Hughes (pages 16–17),
Rhodri Jones (pages 22–23 and back cover), Sean Sprague (pages 26–27) and Penny Tweedie (pages 18–19).

The book begins on page 6.

First published in Great Britain in 2006 by
Frances Lincoln Children's Books, 4 Torriano Mews, Torriano Avenue, London NW5 2RZ

www.franceslincoln.com

British Library Cataloguing in Publication Data available on request

ISBN 1-84507-554-4

Printed in China

1 3 5 7 9 8 6 4 2

Oxfam GB will receive a 4% royalty for each copy of this book sold in the UK.

Bicycles

Kate Petty

FRANCES LINCOLN CHILDREN'S BOOKS
in association with

 Oxfam

Linh can ride his mother's bike but it is much too big for him. The road that runs through his village in Vietnam is very busy.

I'm not allowed to ride on the road yet.

Lucy and her family are going for a bike ride today. This cycle trail in the United Kingdom used to be a railway track.

One day Lucy will ride a bike on her own!

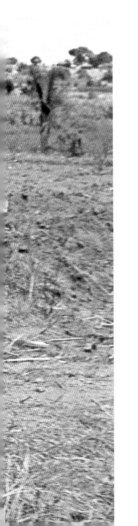

Grandma Rose from Malawi
has a cow and a bike.
She is cycling to market
to sell a full churn of milk.

It's easier
to carry heavy
things on
a bike.

Cidinha has plenty of room to play. She lives next door to the football pitch in her village in Brazil. She is using a bicycle wheel like a hoop.

It's fun to keep the wheel rolling.

Mumi and her friend
live in Java, Indonesia.
They are fixing her bicycle
chain which has come off
on the bumpy road.

I will put
some oil on it
when I get
home.

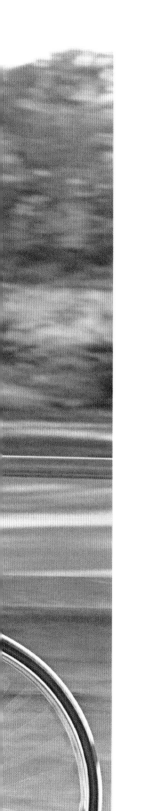

These three boys are coming home from school in Kenya. They are travelling across the river on a taxi-bike.

This is the quickest way home!

Alexis lives in Alice Springs in the Australian outback. She has a big family, so it's good to get away on her mountain bike sometimes.

Mountain bikes are great in the bush.

Kamalotas likes to ride her bike with her dad at weekends. It's a good way of finding out more about her home town in Thailand.

It's nice and shady in this lane.

Dramane can't wait to mend his bicycle. He lives in Mali, where there is lots of space to ride around.

This bike was a present from my dad.

Lots of the children ride their bikes to this school in Cambodia. They arrive really early – in time to eat breakfast before lessons.

I cycled here with my friends.

Tomasa has a good use for a bicycle! She uses it to spin thread for weaving. She belongs to a group of weavers in Guatemala.

The money I earn will buy a new dress.

United
Kingdom

Guatemala

Mali

Brazil

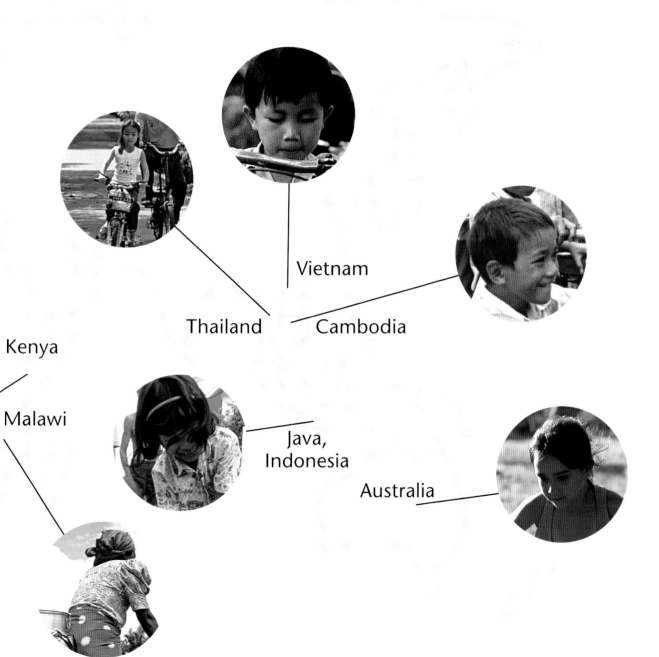

Vietnam

Thailand   Cambodia

Kenya

Malawi

Java,
Indonesia

Australia

MORE BOOKS IN THE AROUND THE WORLD SERIES
FROM FRANCES LINCOLN

HAIR
Kate Petty
In association with Oxfam

We wear our hair in lots of different ways. Sometimes it is
to keep cool. Sometimes it is to look nice for a special occasion.
This book has photographs from all around the world
of some wonderful hairstyles.

PLAYTIME
Kate Petty
In association with Oxfam

Every child enjoys playtime and has a favourite toy or game.
This book looks at photographs of children from all around the world
having fun playing alone or with their friends.

HOME
Kate Petty
In association with Oxfam

Wherever we live in the world, there is always somewhere
we call home. This book looks at the homes of children from
all over the world, who live with their families and sometimes
their whole communities.

Frances Lincoln titles are available from all good bookshops.
You can also buy book and find out more about your favourite titles,
authors and illustrators on our website: www.franceslincoln.com